Everything You Need to Know | *If You and Your Parents Are New Americans*

New American citizens pledge their allegiance to the United States at a citizenship ceremony.

Everything You Need to Know *If You and Your Parents Are New Americans*

Edward J. Santos

The Rosen Publishing Group, Inc.
New York

To Myroka José

Published in 2002 by The Rosen Publishing Group, Inc.
29 East 21st Street, New York, NY 10010

Copyright © 2002 by The Rosen Publishing Group, Inc.

First Edition

All rights reserved. No part of this book may be reproduced in any form without permission in writing from the publisher, except by a reviewer.

Library of Congress Cataloging-in-Publication Data

Santos, Edward J.
Everything you need to know if you and your parents are new Americans/Edward J. Santos. — 1st ed.
p. cm. — (The need to know library)
Includes bibliographical references and index.
ISBN   978-1-4358-8841-8
1. United States—Emigration and immigration—Juvenile literature. 2. Acculturation—United States—Juvenile literature. [1. United States—Emigration and immigration.]
I. Title. II. Series.
JV6543 .S26 2001
304.8'73—dc21

2001002514

Manufactured in the United States of America

Contents

	Introduction	6
Chapter 1	America: Land of Immigration	8
Chapter 2	Coming to America	19
Chapter 3	Fitting In	27
Chapter 4	Hanging On to Your Heritage	36
Chapter 5	Immigrant Parents and American Kids	47
	Glossary	55
	Where to Go for Help	57
	For Further Reading	61
	Index	63

Introduction

Over the centuries, immigrants have come to America for many reasons. Some people hoped to find better jobs. Others wanted to escape poverty, disease, or the devastation of war. There are those who leave their home countries because they are persecuted for their political or religious beliefs or for expressing their ideas. Some people make the journey to be reunited with loved ones who have already moved. And then there are those who are seduced by the American way of living.

Currently, the United States opens its doors to more immigrants each year than any other nation. In doing so, it continues a long tradition as a land of hope and opportunity. A downside of this tradition is that sometimes there are conflicts between these "newer" Americans and those who have lived here longer. In the past, such conflicts have led to discrimination, hate crimes, riots, and even the passing of government laws that were intended to keep immigrants out of the country.

Introduction

Ellis Island

By the late 1800s, with so many immigrants coming to America, the government was having trouble keeping track of all newcomers. To solve this problem, in 1892 a special port of entry was opened in New York's harbor: Ellis Island. On busy days, close to 2,000 immigrants passed through its doors. And by the time it closed, in 1954, more than 20 million immigrants had entered the United States through this port. Today, some 50 percent of all Americans have ancestors who passed through Ellis Island.

Nonetheless, this incredible mixture of people has made the United States a culturally rich and varied place that, in general, is open to new ways. Immigrants built this nation. Their courage, resourcefulness, and independence have become typically American values. The earliest settlers who colonized New England and those who traveled across the untamed countryside to the West are thought of as pioneers of a new land. Every year, the thousands of new Americans who arrive continue to keep this great tradition alive.

Chapter 1
America: Land of Immigration

Leaving behind one's family and friends, language, traditions, and culture to start a new life in a strange place is often an extremely hard decision to make. Yet ever since the first European settlers landed at Plymouth Rock in 1620, millions of people have had the courage to do just that.

You probably know that the first immigrants to settle in America were the English pilgrims who founded the Plymouth Plantation in Massachusetts, in 1620. During this era, much of Europe was experiencing a period of instability that led to frequent wars, which were often fought over religious beliefs. At the time, many new Protestant sects were being created and followers were often punished for their beliefs. In contrast, the vast, unsettled wilds of the New World beckoned as a safe refuge where these persecuted groups could practice their faith without opposition.

America's Very First Immigrants

As you probably know, Christopher Columbus was the first European on record to sail across the Atlantic and "discover" America back in 1492. But Columbus didn't really discover America. Migration to the continent began over 20,000 years ago, when wandering tribes hunting for food followed animal herds across a bridge of land that connected the northern point of Asia with Alaska. These people, who settled North and South America, are the only "native" Americans. By the time Columbus arrived, there were one million Native Americans living in the area that later became the United States. Today, their descendants make up only 0.6 percent of the total population.

Most of America's first colonies were founded by people who were seeking religious freedom. Maryland was founded in 1632 as a colony where English Catholics could live and worship in peace. Jews found refuge in the colonies of New York, Pennsylvania,

On January 24, 1848, gold was found at Sutter's Mill, California, touching off the gold rush. It lured millions to settle the western regions of the country.

Maryland, and Rhode Island, while Quakers and German Protestant sects, such as the Amish and Mennonites, settled peaceful communities in Pennsylvania. The success of these religious communities living side by side led to the right to religious freedom that was included in the Bill of Rights when the new American states achieved independence from England.

Aside from religious freedom, for early newcomers an even bigger draw was the promise of economic prosperity. For the first settlers, America was a vast source of wealth, ranging from good farmland and endless forests of timber to precious gold. Dreams of riches

America: Land of Immigration

opened up the West as gold-seekers, adventurers, pioneers, missionaries, and settlers moved across the often savage country. Along the way, these immigrants literally built America, clearing forests, digging canals, cultivating land, and laying railroad tracks. Though times were tough, with courage and hard work these newcomers who started out with nothing often achieved their dreams of success on their own terms.

The Nineteenth Century

In the nineteenth century, the U.S. government was so eager to attract immigrants to the newly settled Midwest and Western states that it created programs to encourage newcomers to live there. One of the most important was the Homestead Act of 1862, which gave 160 acres of land, for free, to anyone who lived on it for five years and made improvements to it, such as farming or building a home on the land. These programs attracted many immigrants from Germany and Scandinavia.

As land was settled, towns and cities sprung up, along with roads and railroads. The railroads themselves were a big magnet for immigration. Thousands of poor Chinese workers sailed across the Pacific to work at dynamiting land and laying tracks. Poverty-stricken immigrants from England, Ireland, and France followed suit. These railroads succeeded in completely opening up the West for settlement.

Before anti-immigration feelings gained strength, Chinese laborers came to America to work on building the railroads.

However, in the 1870s, the United States suffered a serious economic depression. Americans who were suddenly laid off from their jobs or who were unable to find work blamed the new immigrants for taking away job opportunities that they felt were rightfully theirs. The anti-immigration feeling was so strong that in 1875 the United States government passed an anti-immigration law, which prohibited "undesirables" such as convicts from entering the country. Shortly after, in 1882, Congress passed the Chinese Exclusion Act, which prohibited Chinese workers from immigrating.

Immigrants disembarking at Ellis Island outside of New York City. It is estimated that about half of all Americans have an ancestor who arrived at Ellis Island.

At the same time, the Industrial Revolution had hit the East Coast. New factories and businesses created a wealth of new jobs and opportunities that were grabbed up by immigrants who poured in from Europe. In the big cities, immigrants from the same countries stuck together in their own neighborhoods. After all, it was easier to settle into a new place when you had family and friends from your homeland, and you could speak your own language. Those who came first helped newcomers find homes and jobs. They opened up restaurants and stores where other immigrants could find items from their countries of origin.

The Statue of Liberty

"Give me your tired, your poor, your huddled masses yearning to breathe free.

The wretched refuse of your teeming shore.

Send these, the homeless tempest-tossed to me.

I lift my lamp beside the golden door!"

These famous words by the poet Emma Lazarus are engraved on the base of the Statue of Liberty. The landmark statue that rises up out of New York's harbor—a gift from France—was frequently the first glimpse many immigrants had of America. Recognized throughout the world, it has become a symbol of the hope, freedom, and new beginnings that America offers to those who arrive in search of a better life.

The Statue of Liberty has welcomed immigrants to New York Harbor since October 28, 1886.

The Twentieth Century

At the same time that Lady Liberty's torch welcomed the "huddled masses" to the United States, some American-born citizens began worrying that the United States wouldn't be able to absorb so many new Americans. Between 1890 and 1920, over 18 million immigrants landed in the United States.

Around this time, the U.S. government began to pass laws that outlawed certain types of immigrants. Beggars, convicts, anarchists, the mentally challenged, people with serious diseases, and children without at least one parent were some of those who were turned away. Congress also tried to pass a law prohibiting

If You and Your Parents Are New Americans

entrance to immigrants who couldn't read or write as well as those of "inferior" races. However, President Grover Cleveland refused to approve any such laws. He pointed out that recently "the same thing was said of immigrants who, with their descendants, are now numbered among our best citizens."

During the Great Depression, immigration decreased. During much of the 1930s, one out of every four Americans was unemployed. However, after World War II America grew to be very prosperous. At the same time, the country began opening its doors to a new wave of immigrants: refugees.

Refugees Welcome

The first refugees to come to the United States were Europeans. In 1956, many Hungarians sought refuge in the United States after the Soviet Union's Communist army invaded Hungary. In 1959, close to a million Cubans crossed the narrow strip of ocean separating the two countries—many in tiny boats—to escape the Communist takeover of Cuba by Fidel Castro. America has a long history of taking in refugees forced to escape their countries because of war or political persecution. Each year the government decides from which countries the United States will admit refugees. People are admitted on an individual basis once it has been proven that their lives are in danger.

America: Land of Immigration

Nuevos Americanos, Nuevas Linguas

Today, it is increasingly common to walk down the street of many American cities and hear Spanish spoken. This is hardly surprising considering that close to twenty million new Americans come from Hispanic, or Spanish-speaking, countries. Fifty years ago, there were less than four million. Roughly half of Hispanic Americans come from Mexico and live in the states of California and Texas.

Immigration Quotas

In 1965, President Lyndon B. Johnson signed a law that radically changed American immigration policy. Up until then, certain quotas favored immigrants from northern and western Europe. Under the new law, however, there was no favoritism according to country of origin, race, or religion. Every year, a predetermined number of immigrants are allowed into the United States. New Americans are accepted on a first-come, first-serve basis.

If You and Your Parents Are New Americans

This law has made America a much richer, more dynamic, and more interesting place. Before the 1960s, two-thirds of legal immigrants came from Canada and western Europe. By the 1990s, the biggest number of new Americans were coming from Mexico, the Philippines, Vietnam, the Dominican Republic, Korea, China, India, Russia, Jamaica, and Iran.

Meeting a Tough Challenge with Optimism, Courage, and Hard Work

Believing that they can change their lives for the better, new Americans are optimistic. Arriving in a new place where everything from the food and culture to the language and climate is different, they meet these challenges head-on. Adaptable, quick to learn, and ready to work hard to achieve their goals, these immigrants have made America a land of opportunity where dreams can, and do, become reality. It is little wonder that these attributes, shared by the millions who have come to America over the years, have become character traits of Americans themselves. Ultimately, new Americans *are* America.

Chapter 2
Coming to America

"I came to the United States when I was twelve from El Salvador. Me, my mom, and my two brothers received a letter from my father who had already been living in Florida for two years. Before I came I had to go to immigration in El Salvador. I had a complete medical checkup to make sure I had no diseases. Then I went to the 'questioning' room where I had to answer questions about my whole family and me. Saying good-bye to my friends and my grandparents was the saddest thing. I don't know when I will see them again."

—Silvio, fourteen years old

If You and Your Parents Are New Americans

Who Gets In and Who Doesn't

Each year the government decides how many immigrants it will allow to enter the United States. Under the Immigration Act of 1990, the maximum number of immigrants allowed into the country each year is 700,000. However, this law also takes into account many other exceptions. For instance, there is no limit to the number of immediate family members of U.S. citizens that can immigrate. Refugees are not included in this quota. Neither are people who, while visiting the United States, ask for asylum. People who ask for asylum fear that returning to their countries could place them in danger.

Because many American businesses are always looking for talented people with useful skills, professionals from all over the world are often invited to the United States in order to do specific jobs. So are entrepreneurs who promise to invest money and create new businesses that will employ American workers. People from countries with low immigration rates to the United States are also given priority. Every year, thousands of "diversity visas" are offered to citizens of countries such as Egypt, Peru, Bangladesh, and Pakistan.

Mikhail Baryshnikov

One of the most famous ballet dancers in the world, Mikhail Baryshnikov, was born in Latvia and began

Ballet dancer Mikhail Baryshnikov defected to the United States in search of artistic freedom.

dancing at age twelve. At the age of fifteen, he moved to Leningrad (today St. Petersburg) and studied ballet at one of Russia's top ballet schools. At age nineteen, he joined the distinguished Kirov Ballet and became a star.

However, at the time, Russia—then part of the Soviet Union—was ruled by a very strict Communist regime that controlled every aspect of life, even ballet. Baryshnikov grew increasingly unhappy because he wasn't given any artistic freedom and he was forbidden to live and work outside of his country. Because of this, one night while the Kirov Ballet was touring Canada in 1974, instead of getting on the bus with the other dancers after a show, the twenty-six-year-old dancer defected.

If You and Your Parents Are New Americans

Speeding off in a hired car, he came to America and requested asylum. Within weeks, he was dancing on American stages. In the years since, he has contributed enormously to American ballet and modern dance.

Welcome to America

It doesn't matter why you and your family came to America: whether to escape persecution or poverty, to seek a better life, to join the rest of your family, or to have more education and job opportunities. It also doesn't matter how you came to America: whether it was on a tiny, crowded boat from Haiti or Cuba or a jumbo jet from halfway around the world. The one thing that is certain is that the minute you set foot on American soil, you will be starting a whole new life. Everything will be different and there will be many new things to learn and get used to.

"Driving home from the airport, everything seemed so enormous and very clean. At the same time, I missed all the colors and smells of Africa. When we got to our apartment, there was nothing to sit on. We had to eat dinner on a packing crate and there was no TV. My father was working in construction. My mother stayed at home with my sisters and me. At first, we were lonely. My mother cried a lot and I tried to comfort her. I pointed out that in Odienné, where we lived, she had never had a bathtub or an

Coming to America

electric oven or even a telephone. Except for my father, none of us spoke any English. Because it was winter, we stayed inside the house. I liked watching the snow though. I had never seen snow in my life. In the Ivory Coast, there is no winter."

—*Veronique, fourteen years old*

It is likely that you and your family will experience conflicting emotions when you arrive in America. You will probably miss familiar things and your friends and family members back home. On the other hand, America will probably seem like an exciting place that is full of brand-new things to discover. Feeling happy and sad, lonely and excited, lost and thrilled all at the same time can be very confusing.

This is an important time to stick together as a family. As a teenager, you can play an important role in helping your family adapt to your new life. While your parent(s) are dealing with the stress of new jobs and a new language (as well as juggling important chores ranging from finding a place to live and buying new furniture to opening bank accounts) and dealing with legal requirements of immigration, there are things that you can do to help make this transition easier. Shopping for food, preparing meals, cleaning up, and taking care of younger siblings are just a few examples.

If You and Your Parents Are New Americans

Your Role

Along with helping out your parent(s), you may find that your younger brothers and sisters also need your aid. It is natural for them to feel frightened or overwhelmed by the changes going on in their lives. As their more mature and adaptable older brother or sister, you can offer them comfort and guidance. Help them feel more secure in their new environment by spending time with them and trying to teach them things about the American way of life. Explore your new neighborhood together and check out all the different kinds of delicious foods there are to eat. Practice playing baseball in the park. Help them to understand the lyrics to a song on the radio or to figure out a difficult piece of homework. Take a walk in a park and point out flowers or animals that are new to you. Listen to the new sounds of your city or town. When you think of it, aside from feeling homesick or displaced, this is a new adventure.

Because you have fewer responsibilities than do your parent(s), it will probably be easier for you to meet new people and pick up American ways of doing things. Sometimes, it might be tough to find yourself saddled with extra responsibilities. However, lending a hand at this important moment in your family's life can be a great opportunity to prove yourself—both as a mature and dependable member of your family and as a resourceful new American.

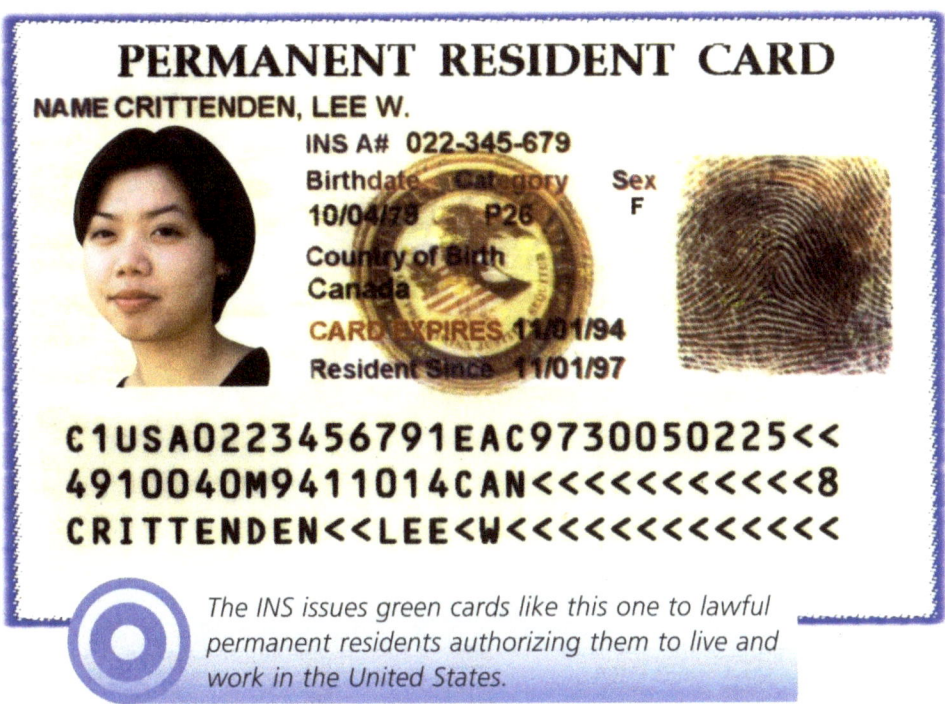

The INS issues green cards like this one to lawful permanent residents authorizing them to live and work in the United States.

The Green Card That Isn't Green

Although you may never have seen a green card, you've probably heard of one. Perhaps you've even seen *Green Card*, the movie about a French man who marries an American woman in order to get one of these precious documents.

A green card is the nickname given to the alien registration receipt card issued by the U.S. government's Immigration and Naturalization Service (INS). These cards are given to aliens—non-American citizens, not people from another planet—when they enter the United States after first having obtained permission to

If You and Your Parents Are New Americans

legally immigrate. Such aliens are known as lawful permanent residents (LPR). LPRs are not American citizens, but they do have the right to live and work here for an indefinite period of time.

When green cards were first issued in 1940, they actually were green. However, because they were so valuable, many people tried to counterfeit them. To prevent this, the INS changed their design and color many times. Over the years, green cards have been pale blue, dark blue, and pink, but to those who want, receive, issue, and inspect them, they have always remained "green cards." The name refers not only to the document itself, but to the official status desired by so many legal non-immigrants (temporary workers, students, and tourists—all of whom can legally remain in the United States for only limited amounts of time) and undocumented aliens (those who enter and remain in the United States illegally).

Today, machine-readable green cards are much more difficult to counterfeit. However, they are still extremely valuable. It is impossible to legally get a job, for instance, without showing your green card to an employer. Whether you and your family are inside or outside of the United States, applying and waiting to receive (or not receive) a green card can sometimes be a complicated, stressful, and long experience.

Chapter 3

Fitting In

"My first day of school, I was so scared. I worried that I wasn't wearing the right clothes and that I didn't look 'normal.' I had taken English courses while I was still in Brazil, and intensive ESL classes with my family here in America, but my speaking was still shaky. When the teacher introduced me to the class, all the kids stared at me and I felt embarrassed. I worried that I'd be behind compared to the other kids and that the teacher would think I was dumb. Later, some kids talked to me, but I was so nervous about my English coming out all funny that I didn't say much. After a while, I found it easier to talk one-on-one, but when I was in a group, everybody talked so fast that I couldn't understand a lot.

If You and Your Parents Are New Americans

> *"Luckily, I am a really good soccer player. Americans like soccer, but it's not such a big thing like it is in Brazil. When I joined the school team, I gained back some confidence in myself. All the other guys and even the coach wanted me to give them tips about Brazilian soccer techniques. Being part of the team allowed me to be me. I ended up making a lot of friends. There were even a couple of girls interested in me."*
>
> —Alberto, fifteen years old

Language Arts

One of the most frustrating things is being in a place and not speaking the language very well. You feel left out of conversations, you can't express your feelings, and you can't understand the jokes that everyone is laughing at. You make mistakes that make you feel stupid. Or you're so afraid of making them that you don't say anything at all, and people think that you are shy, boring, or stuck-up. Sometimes, it feels that the true you is locked inside of a cage and can't get out. It can be frustrating if you used to be the class clown and now you can't even make a wisecrack, or if you used to write really good essays and now your work comes back from the teacher covered with red circles around all your errors.

Fitting In

And sometimes the English language makes no sense at all. After all, why are "book" and "food" pronounced differently? And what about "bow" as in "bow tie" and "bow" as in "take a bow"?

Going to school, taking extra classes, hanging out with new friends, and participating in new activities are all great ways of immersing yourself in the language. If you want to improve you language skills and learn more about American culture—which will allow you to figure out what the kids at school are talking about when they refer to macaroni and cheese, Katie Holmes, Tiger Woods, *Seventeen* magazine, or *Catcher in the Rye*—try to do some of the following in your spare time:

1. Join a video rental store and rent different types of films (such as adventure, suspense, drama, comedy, and documentaries).

2. Read newspapers and magazines. This is a great way to learn what's going on in the United States, in every aspect, from economics to the arts. Many magazines geared especially to teens will give you some insights into the lives of young Americans, as well as offering advice and tips.

If You and Your Parents Are New Americans

3. Join your local library. You can borrow books, videos, magazines, and CDs for free. Reading books and listening to CDs are great ways to pick up new words and discover the variety of American music.

4. Surf the Internet. There are countless Web sites in English on the Net. Listen to interviews. Join a chat room. Read about subjects that interest you.

5. Watch television (in moderation). Like anywhere, there is a lot of junk on American TV, but there are also many interesting programs. TV is an important part of American culture, and especially teen culture, and can be fun and informative. However, while TV can give you a lot of information about American society, be aware that many situations on television shows may seem to be based on reality, but are ultimately fiction. Don't jump to the conclusion that what you see on TV is the way America really is or that the characters that you are

Fitting In

> watching are representative of how most Americans behave.

Similarities and Differences

For any teenager, anywhere in the world, adolescence is a time of change. All teens worry about fitting in. And it's very common for teenagers to want more independence from their parent(s), to be faced with pressures from their peers, to be concerned about being sexually attractive, and to be faced with doubts about who they are and what they want. Take comfort in the fact that, no matter where you come from, you are not alone. In terms of the things that really count, you probably have more in common with your new peers than you think.

Assimilation

It is normal for teens to feel insecure. As a child, you probably spent a lot of time with your family. Your most important references were your parent(s), or closest relatives, who share your background, culture, history, and values. As an adolescent, however, you are probably spending a lot more time with people your own age. Teens—and especially American teens who, because of America's enormous immigrant population, are an exceptionally diverse bunch—are suddenly exposed to other ways of being, behaving, and living. These new experiences may be both scary and interesting.

It is OK to want to fit in with your peers, so you may find yourself acting more "American."

It is natural to want to be part of a group. Because you and your family have chosen to live in America, it is normal that you will be influenced by and want to adopt certain American styles of talking, dressing, and acting. "Assimilation" means absorbing the ways of a new and dominant culture or group. Assimilation, to a certain extent, is essential if you are going to get along with and be happy with the people around you.

However, it's one thing to adapt to certain ways of living: learning to look people in the eye, to shake hands or hug when you say hello or good-bye, and to wear sneakers and jeans. It is a whole other thing to feel pressured—whether by yourself or your peers—into turning your back on your culture and beliefs just to be one of the gang.

Fitting In

In the United States, there is no law saying that you can't wear a prayer cap or a turban or that you have to love baseball, Elvis Presley, and hamburgers with ketchup and mustard. Don't let anybody tell you or make you think that you have to change who you are to fit in. Being American is all about having the courage to be an independent individual with the freedom to express yourself, while being tolerant enough to accept that others have the right to do the same.

Racism and Discrimination

Although in general Americans are tolerant and accepting of difference, unfortunately it is not uncommon to encounter racists who discriminate against people because of race, religion, culture, or skin color. By law, racial and ethnic discrimination is illegal. An employer cannot refuse to hire someone because he or she is a Muslim. A school or university cannot turn away a student because he or she is a Japanese American. Sadly, however, some people do feel threatened by difference, and this fear takes the form of racist attitudes. These attitudes often are expressed in insults or hateful remarks. In some case, they take the form of violent aggression.

If you or anyone in your family is the victim of racial discrimination, go to the police. Receiving hate mail, being threatened, or getting beat up because of

If You and Your Parents Are New Americans

your race is a crime. There is absolutely no reason for you to accept any kind of racist persecution. As a legal resident—and as a human being—you have as much right to be in this country as anybody. And no matter what color your skin is or what faith you believe in, you are as American as anybody else is.

Four (Completely False and Racist) Myths About Immigration

Myth No. 1: America is being invaded by immigrants.

The Reality
Although there are more immigrants living in the United States than ever before, the percentage of immigrants is much smaller than it has been in the past.

Myth No. 2: Immigrants take jobs away from Americans.

The Reality
Immigrants actually create jobs. New Americans are more likely to start new businesses or be self-employed. Small businesses—close to 20 percent of which are started by immigrants—account for 80 percent of the new jobs created in the United States every year.

Fitting In

Myth No. 3: Immigrants are a drain on the American economy.

The Reality
All together, new Americans earn $240 billion a year, pay $90 billion a year in taxes, and receive only $5 billion in welfare. In fact, immigrants are much more likely to have jobs, save more money, and start new businesses than native-born Americans.

Myth No. 4: Immigrants aren't interested in becoming part of American society.

The Reality
Studies indicate the opposite. In fact, parent(s) and grandparent(s) of immigrant kids sometimes worry that their children are assimilating too quickly. Studies show that there are far too few ESL (English as a second language) courses for the number of new Americans eager to take them. And most bilingual children of immigrants prefer to speak English than their mother tongue.

Chapter 4
Hanging On to Your Heritage

"Both of my parents are Korean, but I was born and grew up here in the United States. My parents speak English to each other and most of their friends aren't Asian Americans. And yet, on Sundays we always drive to the Korean part of town to eat dinner and to check out the stores. I love Korean food and I am always bugging my mom to make it. I bring some whenever my school has Multicultural Day. A couple of the kids make funny faces and hold their noses. They think that kimchee smells funny or that the textures are weird, but they don't know what they're missing. Every Saturday, I go to Korean school and I can speak pretty well. When I graduate from high school, I'm going to spend a year in Korea teaching English."

—Michael, thirteen years old

A Cuban American girl turns "sweet sixteen." As an immigrant and an American, you can embrace both your home culture and your new culture.

Whether you came to this country with one or both parents as a child or you are the American-born son or daughter of one or two immigrant parents, as a new American, you are in a privileged position. Like many young people in your situation, you have automatic access to at least two, and possibly more, cultures.

Keeping Your Culture

Growing up and living in America means that you don't have to choose between being Mexican or American, Vietnamese or American, or Ethiopian or American. In the United States, you are allowed to be a Mexican American, a Vietnamese American, or an

Suppressing your culture is like denying or neglecting a part of yourself. You should never forget your heritage.

Ethiopian American, and because of this, you are free to take the best elements of both cultures and make them into your own particular identity. However, as we saw in the previous chapter, sometimes the pressure to assimilate and become "all-American" can be stronger than the ties that bind you to your family's original roots. Hanging on to your heritage is not always easy. And at a certain point in time, it might not even seem that important. That's why it's important to remember that suppressing or neglecting your past and where you come from is like destroying a part of yourself.

Hanging On to Your Heritage

Melting Pot Versus Patchwork Quilt

For a long time, the United States was known as a melting pot. Immigrants who arrived in America were eager to have their origins melt away in order to become part of a big, new, and universal "Americanized" culture. America was seen as a big pot of soup, with different flavors produced by different cultures, but with one main taste.

In many ways, this view has changed. Since the 1960s, different ethnic groups within America, ranging from Native Americans and African Americans to Croatian Americans and Asian Americans, have proudly asserted their distinct identities. Today, America is often compared instead to a patchwork quilt: a constantly changing and growing fabric made up of peoples who, while remaining unique, work together like the pieces of a quilt to form a complex but united whole.

If You and Your Parents Are New Americans

Bilingualism

To grow up speaking a language other than English—either because you lived in another country or because, in America, your parent(s) or other relatives speak their mother tongue—is a great gift. Being bilingual—meaning that you can communicate fluently in two languages (if you can speak more than two, you are multilingual)—offers numerous advantages. It means that you can read books, see films, listen to music, and have access to a wealth of information in two different languages.

Being bilingual also means that you can travel to your country of origin and communicate with friends and strangers alike. It gives you the chance of forging new relationships and bonds. If you are lucky enough to speak a language such as Spanish, French, Arabic, or Portuguese, vast parts of the globe open up to you. A bilingual Cuban American will have no trouble getting around in Argentina or Nicaragua, just as a Tahitian American will be able to make him or herself understood in Haiti, Mali, or Québec.

Furthermore, with the world becoming increasingly globalized, the more languages you speak, the more job opportunities become available. Careers in sectors ranging from business and communications to translation and education all value people with multiple languages. As American companies expand around the world and foreign companies move into the United

You should appreciate the chance to be bilingual. Learning a second language can bring you great opportunities.

States, the possibilities of finding high-paid and interesting jobs are limitless.

For these reasons, don't turn your back on the chance of being bilingual. Ask your parent or another family member to speak with you in your native language. Go to the library and check out foreign language books, videos, and other media. Find out from your local ethnic association or cultural center about after-school or weekend language courses. Enrolling in such courses will also allow you to meet other new Americans who not only share your background, but who may also be facing the same experiences, concerns, or problems as you are. Finally, if you can, spend a period of time in

If You and Your Parents Are New Americans

your country of origin, where you can immerse yourself in both the language and the culture. Not only will such a trip vastly improve your language skills, it will also motivate you to want to speak the language.

Religion

In terms of religion, America is one of the most tolerant countries in the world. As seen in chapter 1, this nation was created as a haven where people were free to practice whatever faith they wanted without persecution. Today, American cities are filled with churches, synagogues, mosques, temples, and other places of worship.

Although Americans believe in many different religions, the dominant faith is Christianity. Had you grown up in Israel, many of your friends would have been Jewish, or had you grown up in Turkey, you would have been surrounded mainly by Muslims. However, in America, unless you are living in a tightly knit ethnic community, many of your peers will tend to be Christian.

Some people find it tough to live through Christmas and Easter with all the commercial and media hype that accompanies them. If your family doesn't celebrate these holidays, you may feel left out. At the same time, if you are Muslim, you might feel singled out when you take time off from school to fast for Ramadan. However, living in America doesn't mean giving up

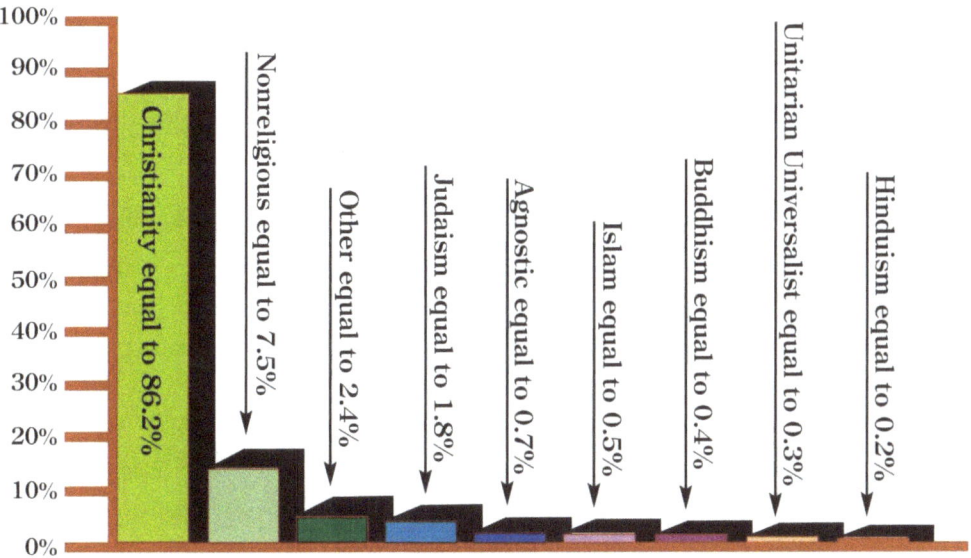

Religion and Estimated Percentage of Adult Population

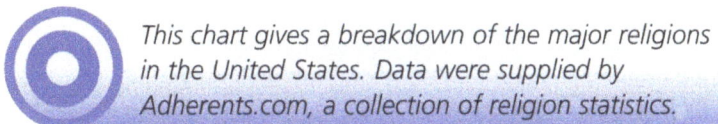

This chart gives a breakdown of the major religions in the United States. Data were supplied by Adherents.com, a collection of religion statistics.

your spiritual beliefs. Your religion is something that transcends your geographical location. It is part of the values that your family has handed down to you. It is part of where you come from, so celebrate your heritage instead of worrying about being different.

Religion is often not just about belief; it is about a sense of community. Many new Americans find comfort in religion because its offshoots—worship, rituals, meals, and ceremonies—bring them together with others from the same background. In doing so, they are preserving more than a belief; they are preserving a whole way of life.

If You and Your Parents Are New Americans

Even if you don't agree with all aspects of your family's religion, as long as you live with your parent(s) and are a part of their family, you should at least respect their beliefs. When you become an adult, you will be free to practice whatever you want. Maybe you will be a Buddhist or a Mormon. Maybe—if you have parent(s) of two religious backgrounds—you will practice two religions, a mixture of two, or something entirely different. Ultimately, religion is a very personal and spiritual choice that only you can make.

Culture

Culture refers to a set of beliefs, customs, habits, and ways of behaving that are shared by a certain group of people. Most countries have their own distinct cultures. For instance, drinking wine is an important part of Italian culture. The French like to eat cheese at the end of a meal. Dancing the samba is a part of Brazilian culture. Even within countries, there are specific regional or group cultures. Québec is the only part of Canada in which most people speak French, practice Catholicism, and eat a delicious meat pie called *tourtiere*.

A culture is an organic, or living, thing that is always changing and incorporating other cultures into itself. As globalization occurs, and the world becomes more connected, cultures influence one another. American culture is a mixture of habits brought by different immigrants. Blue jeans actually originated in France, the great

Although you live in a new country, you can feel free to embrace your native culture and traditions, like this bride in traditional Indian wedding garb.

If You and Your Parents Are New Americans

Hollywood studios were founded by eastern and central European Jews, and chili and tacos come from Mexico.

Hold onto Your Roots

Hanging onto the culture from which your family comes is what makes you distinct. Even if you only have one parent or grandparent who was born in and came from another country, that culture is partially yours. It is the food you eat (pad thai, curry, paella, or roast beef), the music you listen to (mazurkas, merengues, tangos), the clothes you wear (saris, bui buis, clogs), the way you treat people (shaking hands, kissing cheeks, opening your house to strangers), the holidays you celebrate (Chinese New Year, Rosh Hashana, Day of the Dead). All of these things might be seen as "different" in the eyes of the "average American," but the state of being "different" is itself American. And once you get past the stereotypes in films and on TV, you begin to realize that there is no such thing as an "average American."

Outside of your family, there are plenty of places to immerse yourself in your culture. Ethnic associations, cultural centers, and places of worship are good places to begin. So are the restaurants, bookstores, theaters, cinemas, and stores that you'll find in ethnic communities or neighborhoods. Because culture is organic, you can pick and choose, mix and match many cultural elements—both from your or your parents' native country and from the multiple aspects of "American" culture.

Chapter 5: Immigrant Parents and American Kids

"I have many friends from Tibet. Some are very 'Americanized.' Others try to teach their children Tibetan values. I worry about my teenage daughter who is now in high school. I allow her to go out with a group of friends of both sexes but I don't want her to date until she's in college. I also don't want her to go to school dances. I came with my family to America when I was fourteen and finished high school here. I didn't go to my prom and I have to admit I felt very left out because I never had this and other typically American high school experiences. I don't want my daughter to feel excluded but I also don't like the sexual pressures that American teens face."

—A Tibetan American mother

Teens may face problems if aspects of their Americanized lifestyle—such as getting a tattoo—conflict with the cultural traditions of their parent(s).

In the previous chapters, we examined some situations encountered by teens who had recently immigrated to America or who had been born outside of the United States but had grown up here. Such teens are known as first-generation Americans. Often their experiences in adapting to American life are different from second-generation and third-generation Americans.

Generation Gaps

Second-generation Americans are those who were born and raised in America, but whose parent(s) were born and raised in their country (or countries) of origin. Third-generation Americans are those whose parent(s)

Immigrant Parents and American Kids

grew up in America, but whose grandparent(s) came from other countries. If you are a second- or third-generation American, you probably feel more assimilated than a first-generation teenager does.

Certain problems might arise when your beliefs and lifestyle and those of your peers conflict with the traditional values and customs of your parent(s) or grandparent(s). Aspects of American teen culture that seem natural to you—dating, tattoos, fast food, wearing ripped jeans—might shock your parent(s) or grandparent(s), who grew up in another place under different rules.

Getting Along at Home

Assimilating into a new culture is probably more complicated for second-generation teens. After all, no matter how "Americanized" you feel or want to be, you live in your parents' home and must abide by their rules. They are responsible for raising you the best way that they know how. What influences them in their decisions is how they themselves were raised and the values that were passed onto them. It would be helpful for you to take this into consideration when you try to convince your mom that you want to go away skiing for the weekend with a bunch of friends or when your dad refuses to let you shave your head. Remember that elements of American culture that seem normal to you don't necessarily seem that way to your parent(s), just as aspects of their culture might seem old-fashioned or strange to you.

The "American way" is not the only way. Your parent(s) may be critical of some things, like fast food, and may instead offer alternatives.

Ultimately, the key is flexibility. Try to keep the channels of communication open. Instead of defiantly announcing that you are going to a Radiohead concert and there's nothing your parent(s) can do to stop you, explain why you want to go and who will be there, and discuss when you will be home. With luck, instead of immediately denying you permission to go, your parent(s) will be open-minded and will listen to you. Even if they decide not to let you go, they will tell you their reasons.

Another thing to keep in mind is that the "American way" is not the only way. Eventually, your parent(s) will come to feel comfortable and will embrace certain elements of American culture. You should be aware that this may take a while. At the same time, your parent(s) may think negatively about certain elements of American culture—the use of guns and the high incidence of gun-related violence, eating too much junk food, a lack of respect toward elderly people, and rampant materialism—and with good reason. Not everything in America is perfect, and your parent(s) might be very justified in criticizing certain things and offering alternative values and ways of behaving.

Building Bridges

Often, many second-generation and third-generation teens feel like yo-yos, caught in the middle between two cultures: the culture of their family and American culture. Some teens feel pulled in two directions. Others feel as if they don't belong completely in either world.

"My parent(s) are Iranian, but I was born here. When I traveled to Iran to visit relatives in Tehran, I felt very out of place. My cousins said

If You and Your Parents Are New Americans

I was weird because I had shaved the hair on my arms and tweezed my eyebrows. They thought I was more American than Iranian because I spoke English better than Farsi. But sometimes in the United States, when I tell people that I'm Muslim they look at me as if I'm a terrorist or something."

—Asminee, sixteen years old

On the positive side, having access to two cultures is very enriching. Instead of feeling like a yo-yo, try feeling like a bridge. If your parent(s) or grandparent(s) are afraid or suspicious of certain elements of American culture, know that it is because they may not have the same understanding of a situation that you do. Instead of passively accepting the situation, take some initiative. Why not be the mediator who introduces your family to things about America that you know better than they do? After all, as a teen you are always meeting new people and are exposed to new things in a manner that your parent(s) aren't. Try taking a parent or relative to movies and museums, introduce them to your friends (and your friends' families), have them get involved in some of the school or extra-curricular activities you do, and encourage them to get involved in some of their own.

If your parent(s) have trouble adjusting to their new home, try taking them to museums to expose them to interesting things about your adopted country.

If You and Your Parents Are New Americans

At the same time, if you feel that your American friends feel slightly timid or uncomfortable about aspects of your family's culture or religion, know that these probably also stem from a lack of knowledge. Once again, take the initiative and build a bridge. Have your parent(s) make a typical meal and invite some friends (and their families) over. Invite them to a traditional religious service or ceremony. Take them on a tour of your ethnic neighborhood or show them pictures of your family's native country. Chances are they will be much more interested than you ever imagined.

As President John F. Kennedy, the grandson of an Irish immigrant, once said: "The secret of America [is that it is] a nation of people with the fresh memory of old traditions who dare to explore new frontiers."

GLOSSARY

anarchist Someone who rebels against governmental authority.
assimilate To absorb the ways of a new and dominant culture or group.
asylum Refuge, protection.
bilingual Mastery of and ability to communicate in two languages.
counterfeit Fake or false.
defect To leave or abandon one place, cause, or ideology for another.
ESL English as a second language courses (English classes for non-native speakers).
ethnic Characteristics specific to a religious, racial, national, or cultural group.

If You and Your Parents Are New Americans

green card Plastic photo identification card given to individuals who become legal permanent residents of the United States.

immerse To plunge into something.

macaroni and cheese Pasta that is mixed with cheese and served as a casserole.

mediator Someone who acts as an intermediary between two groups.

naturalization Act of becoming a citizen of a country.

persecution To attack or harm someone because of their beliefs.

quota A set number of people allowed into a country.

Ramadan Month-long period of fasting according to the Muslim calendar.

refugee Someone forced to leave home to escape war, disease, discrimination, or famine.

Rosh Hashanah Jewish New Year.

second-generation American-born children of immigrants.

third-generation American-born grandchildren of immigrants.

Where to Go for Help

Advocates for Language Learning
P.O. Box 4952
Culver City, CA 90231
(310) 313-3333

American Immigration Center
(800) 814-1555
Web site: http://www.us-immigration.com

Association of MultiEthnic Americans
P.O. Box 66061
Tucson, AZ 85728-6061
(877) 954-AMEA (2632)
Web site: http://www.ameasite.org

If You and Your Parents Are New Americans

ERIC Clearinghouse on Languages and Linguistics
4646 40th Street NW
Washington, DC 20016-1859
(800) 276-9834
Web site: http://www.cal.org/ericll

Immigration History Research Center
University of Minnesota
College of Liberal Arts
311 Andersen Library
222 21st Avenue S
Minneapolis, MN 55455-0439
(612) 625-4800
Web site: http://www1.umn.edu/ihrc

National Latino Children's Institute
320 El Paso Street
San Antonio, TX 78207
(210) 228-9997
Web site: http//www.nlci.org

National Network for Early Language Learning
Center for Applied Linguistics
4646 40th Street NW
Washington, DC 20016-1859
(202) 362-0700
Web site: http://www.educ.iastate.edu/nnell

Where to Go for Help

Web Sites

About Immigration
http://immigration.about.com

Ellis Island Immigration Museum
http://www.ellisisland.org/

Family Tree Maker
Search for family members online and chat with other users on the genealogy message boards.
http://www.familytreemaker.genealogy.com

Foreignborn.com
A Web site for all foreign-born individuals entering or living in the United States.
http://www.foreignborn.com

Immigration—The Journey to America
History of different immigrant groups in America.
http://library.thinkquest.org/20619/Intro.html

Immigration Stories
Mexican and Vietnamese immigrants tell their stories.
http://www.otan.dni.us/webfarm/emailproject/grace.htm

If You and Your Parents Are New Americans

Negative Population Growth (NPG) Population Facts and Figures
Information on U.S. population growth.
http://npg.org/facts.htm

United States Immigration and Naturalization Service (INS)
Information, laws, statistics, and forms about immigration and naturalization.
http://www.ins.usdoj.gov/graphics/index.htm

Web Kids: Immigration Page
All sorts of information for kids about immigration in America.
http://www.cadl.lib.mi.us/webkids/kids/immigration.htm

For Further Reading

Bartoletti, Susan Campbell. *A Coal Miner's Bride: The Diary of Anetka Kaminska*. New York: Scholastic, 2000.

Boswell, Bethanie L. *Speaking Two Languages*. Vero Beach, FL: Rourke Publications, 1995.

Budhos, Marina Tamar. *Remix: Conversations with Immigrant Teenagers*. New York: Henry Holt and Company, 1999.

Cozic, Charles P., ed. *Illegal Immigration: Opposing Viewpoints*. San Diego, CA: Greenhaven Press, 1997.

Freedman, Russell. *Immigrant Kids*. New York: Puffin Books, 1995.

Gillan, Maria Mazziotti. *Growing up Ethnic in America: Contemporary Fiction About Learning to Be American*. New York: Viking Penguin, 1999.

If You and Your Parents Are New Americans

Lawlor, Veronica. *I Was Dreaming to Come to America: Memories from the Ellis Island Oral History Project.* New York: Viking Children's Books, 1995.

Machlin, Mikki. *My Name Is Not Gussie.* Boston: Houghton, Mifflin and Co., 1999.

Strom, Yale. *Quilted Landscapes: Conversations with Young Immigrants.* New York: Simon and Schuster Children's, 1996.

Index

A
American colonies, 8, 9–10
alien registration receipt card, 25–26
anti-immigration laws, 6, 15–16, 17, 20
assimilating, 31–33, 37–38, 49
asylum, 20, 21–22

B
Baryshnikov, Mikhail, 20–22
bilingualism, 40–42
Bill of Rights, 10

C
Chinese Exclusion Act, 12
Columbus, Christopher, 9
culture, 37–38, 44–46

D
defection, 21–22
discrimination, 6, 33–35

E
Ellis Island, 7
English, learning, 28–31
English as a second language, 35

G
generation gap, 48–51
gold rush, 10–11
Great Depression, 16
green card, 25–26

H
hate crimes, 6, 33–34
Homestead Act, 11

I
immigration
 adjusting to, 22–24, 27–35
 African, 20, 22–23
 Asian, 18, 20, 36, 47
 backlash against, 6, 12, 15
 Chinese, 11, 12
 European, 8, 10, 11, 13, 16, 17, 18, 20–21
 Hispanic, 16, 17, 18, 19
 Jewish, 9
 laws, 6, 15–16, 17, 20
 Middle Eastern, 18, 51–52
 nineteenth century, 11–13
 Protestant, 8
 quotas on, 17

railroads and, 11
reasons for, 6, 7, 10–11, 20, 22
second-generation, 48–49
statistics on, 7, 9, 15, 17, 20, 34, 35
third generation, 48–49
twentieth century, 15–18
Immigration and Naturalization Service (INS), 25–26
Industrial Revolution, 13

L
language skills, 28–31, 40–42
lawful permanent residents (LPR), 26

M
melting pot, 39

N
Native Americans, 9
nineteenth century immigration, 11–13

P
persecution, 6, 16, 22

Q
Quakers, 10

R
racism, 6, 16, 33–35
railroads, 11
refugees, 16, 20
religion, 6, 8, 10, 42–44

S
Statue of Liberty, 14, 15

U
undocumented aliens, 26

W
World War II, 16

About the Author
Edward J. Santos is a writer and teen educator who, in his spare time, plays drums and composes music. He lives with his wife, three children, and pet snake, in Florida.

Photo Credits
Cover, pp. 2, 10, 12, 13, 15, 21, 45, 48, 50, 53 © Corbis; pp. 25 (green card) © AP/Wide World Photos; pp. 25 (girl), 32 © Index Stock; pp. 37, 41 © The Image Works; p. 38 © FPG. Information in chart on p. 43 supplied by Adherents.com.

Designer
Nelson Sá

www.ingramcontent.com/pod-product-compliance
Lightning Source LLC
Chambersburg PA
CBHW041114070526
44584CB00002B/165